What

This book will seek to provide a concise view of the subject and must therefore necessarily leave out much of the detail that can be truly fascinating. A few key events or people will be more closely examined to offer a fuller understanding of some of the issues. Should you wish to delve deeper into the subject there is a suggested further reading list at the end of this book.

I am not a professional historian. I am a passionate amateur, but I have always believed that the key to understanding any historical event, period or topic is understanding the people, not least understanding that they were people. Just like you and I they had hopes, dreams, desires, disasters and disappointments that all came together to make the person remembered to history often as a caricature.

This is not a weighty tome; it is an overview of the subject offering some key details and information. I do not frequently reference source material to avoid making the matter thicker than this view is designed to be.

I hope that you will enjoy reading this book as much as I have enjoyed writing it.

Why This Book?

The first thing to do is to put my hands up and say "I am a Ricardian". I have long been fascinated by him and am a member of the Richard III Society. I say this from the outset and without shame because it is perhaps the most obvious reason for writing this particular book.

Beyond that, though, lies a man so lost in legend that no true form remains in the black shadow history has cast over him. He is only a caricature of evil to many, Shakespeare's hunchbacked, scheming murderer. By digging just a little deeper, such light is shone upon the matter as to shrink the shadow to nought, revealing a man. A very different man from the one that history remembers.

Hopefully by the end of this book you will also see the man, or at least enough of him to decide upon the validity of our collective memory of him, and see how and why that memory came to overshadow the last Plantagenet king.

Contents

1.	The Wars Of The Roses	page ... 7
2.	Born To Be Nobody	page ...11
3.	The Ludlow Effect	page ...13
4.	A Royal Prince	page ...17
5.	The Kingmaker	page ...21
6.	Lord Of The North	page ...25
7.	The French Campaign	page ...31
8.	Lord Protector	page ...35
9.	Bad Blood	page ...41
10.	Buckingham Rebellion	page ...47
11.	Not A Drop Of Doubtful Royal Blood	page ...53
12.	Parliament	page ...57
13.	Personal Disasters	page ...61
14.	The Battle Of Bosworth Field	page ...65
15.	Hornby Castle – The Price Of Power	page ...71
16.	I Am Determined To Prove A Villain	page ...77
17.	Conclusion	page ...83
18.	Further Reading	page ...87

The Wars Of The Roses

The period of sporadic civil conflict that ran from 1455 to, in the estimation of most, 1485 (though this is open to debate), was termed the Wars of the Roses around the nineteenth century and the name is often attributed to the writer Sir Walter Scott. The period saw a dynastic struggle for the Crown of England that devastated the aristocracy, polarising support between the Houses of Lancaster and York. The heraldic symbol of the House of Lancaster was the red rose, while the House of York took the white rose and it is from this that the idiom was born. At the time the phrase would not have meant anything to the people. It was simply war.

King Edward III died in 1377. His eldest son, the Black Prince, had died the previous year and so Edward's grandson was the new king. Richard II was 10 years old when he came to the throne and his uncles sought to rule for him until he came of age. When he was older, Richard proved deeply unpopular for many reasons and in 1399, his cousin, Henry Bollingbroke, who Richard had exiled, returned and seized the throne as King Henry IV. Henry's father was one of Richard's uncles, John of Gaunt, Duke of Lancaster and so Henry IV became the first Lancastrian king. Henry IV was succeeded in 1413 by his son, the glorious King Henry V of Agincourt renown and it must have seemed that the Lancastrian kings were secure and set to flourish.

Henry V died suddenly of dysentery on campaign in France in 1422. His son was only nine months old when he became King Henry VI and for many years England was ruled by regents on Henry's behalf. Henry is widely regarded as having been a deeply pious man but unsuited to mediaeval kingship. He suffered from mental health problems and frequent bouts of catatonia when he would not speak or recognise anyone for prolonged periods of time. Despite the reluctance of Henry's wife, Richard, Duke of York was named Protector of the Realm during Henry's illness. Eventually, the Duke of York, the senior noble in the country, was named as Henry's heir to the exclusion of the Prince of Wales, yet the Duke grew impatient and the Wars of the Roses sprouted from the dispute between York and Lancaster for the Crown.

The Duke of York was killed, along with his second son, at the Battle of Wakefield on 30th December 1460. Only a few months later, his eldest son, Edward, Earl of March managed to complete his father's work and became King Edward IV on 4th March 1461. Henry VI was briefly returned to the throne in October 1470 when Edward fell out with his cousin the Earl of Warwick, the Kingmaker. Regaining his throne in April 1471, Edward disposed of Henry after his son had died at the Battle of Tewkesbury. Edward then reigned until 1483 when he died after a short illness, leaving his twelve year old son to become King

Edward V. Edward IV's brother, Richard, Duke of Gloucester was appointed Protector but later became King to the exclusion of his nephew. Richard III lost his Crown and his life at the Battle of Bosworth on 22nd August 1485. The victor was the last Lancastrian hope, Henry Tudor, Earl of Richmond. As King Henry VII, he founded the Tudor dynasty. Henry married Elizabeth of York, daughter of Edward IV, uniting York and Lancaster

Traditionally the Wars of the Roses are viewed as ending at Bosworth, but struggles continued afterwards, including the Battle of Stoke in 1487 and several Pretenders to Henry's throne. Some of the relatives of the House of York were to prove thorns in the Tudor side for a long time to come.

Born To Be Nobody

Richard Plantagenet was born on 2nd October 1452 at Fotheringhay Castle in Northamptonshire. He was the seventh child and fourth son to survive born to Richard Plantagenet, Duke of York and his wife Cecily Neville. As the fourth son, he was unlikely to inherit a great deal and would most likely have been expected to make his own way in the world. A career in the Church was perhaps most likely.

The Duke of York was a great grandson of King Edward III and the most senior noble in England by the time his namesake was born. Cecily was a great, great granddaughter of King Edward III herself through a different branch of the family. Called the Rose of Raby for her beauty, Cecily was a member of the powerful Neville family who held vast authority and influence in the north of England. They were frequently at odds with the Percy family who also held great power in the region.

It was reported later by a Neville family historian, John Rous that Richard was born with shoulder length hair and a full set of teeth after two years in his mother's womb. It is worth noting that Rous wrote this account after Richard's death having praised him greatly during his lifetime. Clearly this account seems unlikely and contemporaries often stated that Richard bore a much greater resemblance to his father than his brothers did. The Duke of York was a man of average looks and normal height, so we can infer that his youngest son was similarly unremarkable.

The Ludlow Effect

In the spring of 1459, aged 6, Richard was moved with his mother and older brother George to Ludlow Castle. As conflict escalated, the Duke of York no longer trusted his family to the defences of Fotheringhay. Ludlow was a seat of Yorkist power in the west. Originally a Neville property the castle was large and its defences stout. Protected by sharp cliffs and the River Teme, it is today a powerful ruin which, in its prime, must have been awesome to behold.

The young Richard would have met his other brothers there. The tall, handsome seventeen year old Edward and the sixteen year old Edmund. Earls in their own right, of March and Rutland respectively, Richard must have been star struck as they practised their martial skills in the castle courtyard. It may even have been the first time that he had met them.

Over the spring and summer the Duke mustered his forces to Ludlow. Toward the end of summer, news arrived that young Richard's uncle the Earl of Salisbury was coming, and so was his son, the famous Earl of Warwick. Warwick was Captain of Calais and his exploits must have been the stuff of legend to a young boy. Salisbury arrived on 25th September and Warwick a few days later with a large portion of the Calais garrison.

In early October, as Richard celebrated his seventh birthday, news arrived that the King's army was approaching the Ludford meadows outside Ludlow where the Yorkist forces were encamped. The Duke protested his loyalty to the King. The King's message that was returned offered a pardon to anyone who deserted York's cause now.

On 12th October, the King's army arrived with Henry VI himself at its head. To the mediaeval mind, taking the field of battle against God's anointed King was inconceivable. A sin. The King's army camped a few miles from Ludford. As night fell, the Calais garrison Warwick had brought scaled the earthworks around the camp and deserted into the darkness and the King's pardon. At a time when the Crown had no standing army, the Calais garrison was the closest to a professional army paid by the Crown that existed. Its loss was a huge blow.

York, Salisbury and Warwick held an emergency council of war. Their decision was probably the only one available to them. They took to their horses and fled. York and his son Edmund headed to Ireland and a rapturous welcome whilst Salisbury, Warwick and Edward made for the Devon coast and then Calais where they dug in, stealing a fleet of royal ships that assembled to assault them in the kind of act that was making Warwick a legend.

The decision in which we are most interested here is that regarding Cecily Neville and her other sons. The Duchess, George and Richard, now just passed a seventh birthday that may have forgone too much celebration, were left behind in Ludlow Castle. In the morning, the King's army descended upon Ludlow.

They found Cecily, with her two young sons, standing alone on the steps of the market cross. The scene is remembered as one of supreme nobility on the part of the Duchess, refusing to cower and hide. For Richard, though, it must have been terrifying. Perhaps Cecily sought to save Ludlow by surrendering willingly, but she did not. As she was hauled to the King with her sons, the army ransacked Ludlow, drinking, stealing and raping until they were sated. The castle was looted of anything of value.

York and his adherents were attainted for treason and their lands forfeit. Cecily, George and Richard were placed into the care of her sister, the Duchess of Buckingham. They were well treated there. The Duke of Buckingham, Humphrey Stafford, was a renowned figure of honour and chivalry who had sought to mediate between his brother-in-law and the King but, when the crunch came, had been unable to break his vows to God's anointed King.

This episode in Richard's life must have had an impact upon him. Thrust into a conflict that he could barely understand and in which his only infraction was being the son of one of the protagonists. He played no part in the events at Ludlow but what he witnessed as a boy of seven must have left its mark. Abandoned by his father and his dashing older brothers, his uncle and his cousin in the night. Left to face an army. Doubtless his mother's actions were noble but how must Richard have felt stood beside her as the rampaging army approached? Frightened? Undoubtedly. Determined not to show it? Perhaps.

He was the son of a Duke and had his mother's example to follow. Did he learn the unfair uncertainty of war that day as he saw Ludlow pillaged like a conquered French town? Did he learn the importance of nobility of action from his brave mother? Did he learn real fear? Did he learn that even family could not be trusted? We shall also return to the Buckingham effect later.

A Royal Prince

Two years after Ludlow, with his father and brother Edmund dead and having served a spell in the Low Countries in the uncomfortable security of exile, Richard's fortunes changed, and his world with them. His brother Edward won. He became King Edward IV and in that instant, on his return to English soil at the age of eight, Richard ceased being a fourth son of a Duke destined for obscurity and became a royal prince. Raised to the Dukedom of Gloucester, Richard was also made a Knight of the Bath and Knight of the Garter.

In line with the tradition of the age, Richard was sent to the household of a noble for his knightly training. Little is known of this period of Richard's life but he spent time at Middleham Castle under the tutelage of his cousin, Richard Neville, Earl of Warwick. Warwick was nephew to Cecily, the son of her brother the Earl of Salisbury and an increasingly powerful noble. He had been powerful as Captain of Calais but his crucial assistance in winning the throne for Edward brought ever more power. It was at Middleham that Richard met Francis Lovell, who was to become a lifelong friend, probably Richard's best friend right until the end.

No record remains of Richard's training regime at Middleham, but it is likely to have included knightly, martial skills with sword, lance and a horse combined with a deeply religious education, learning Latin and reading scripture.

It is believed that it is during this period, around twelve years of age, that Richard began to develop scoliosis, a sideways curvature of the spine. Expert analysis of his skeleton has suggested that he was not born with the condition but developed it during his adolescence. Some contemporary descriptions of Richard as an adult hint at an unevenness in his shoulders but there is no widespread discussion recorded of it. After his death, Shakespeare would pass into legend the hunchback with the withered arm. We can be certain that he was neither, but as a young boy, looking at his vital, 6 foot 4 inch brother the King, the pain that he must have begun to feel as the condition showed itself must have affected him emotionally as well as physically. At a time when physical imperfection was believed to be a signal of moral imperfection, Richard must have known how the world would judge him should his secret be discovered. Did he struggle through the increasing pain his training brought without showing the discomfort? Certainly he was considered extremely pious throughout his life and this may have been influenced by his need to prove that he did not deserve his physical affliction.

Richard, for reasons stated above, never dwelt upon his physical condition and I shall not seek to here either, but it undoubtedly shaped the man that he became and perhaps serves to make his later reputation on the field of battle all the more impressive.

The Kingmaker

Richard Neville, Earl of Warwick has passed into history as The Kingmaker. He played a pivotal role in the changing tides of the Wars of the Roses but also in the development and experiences of his cousin, Richard, Duke of Gloucester. In 1452, Warwick and his father had backed the King against the Duke of York but in mid 1453 Henry VI slipped into one of his catatonic periods. The Duke of Somerset, a favourite of Henry's wife, Margaret of Anjou, became effective leader of the government. Warwick was in dispute with Somerset over a large inheritance and Somerset's rise, along with the disadvantage that it brought to Warwick, caused the Earl to change his allegiance. During the following decade he became central to the Yorkist cause. Warwick gained the title Constable of Calais during one of York's Protectorates and it provided him with a power base that proved vital.

Once Edward was King, Warwick was the most powerful noble in all the land. He was extravagant in the extreme, throwing huge banquets, always one course longer and more expensive than anyone else, including the King. Warwick also set about the most important task for the fledgling regime. He opened negotiations to arrange the marriage of Edward to the daughter of the French King. Edward tended to favour an alliance with Burgundy, France's enemy, but the

Earl pressed on with arrangements, believing that it was the best course for the country, not least because Margaret of Anjou was seeking to marry her son to the same French princess to rebuild and revitalise the Lancastrian threat.

The negotiations were being finalised in 1464 when Edward casually announced to his Privy Council, as though it were some trifling matter that he had forgotten to mention, that he was already married, in secret to a widowed commoner from a Lancastrian family. The open-jawed amazement may have been comical but for the offence that this caused to Warwick. He was embarrassed, both at home and in France, and his honour affronted. His relationship with Edward never recovered. In 1469, after spending nearly an hour on his knees before his old enemy, Warwick was reconciled with Margaret of Anjou and joined her to return Henry VI, who had been a prisoner in the Tower of London for eight years, to the throne. With Warwick's power behind it, the revolt succeeded. Richard was now seventeen and it is here that we can glimpse him again as events unravel, though he is now far from the frightened boy of Ludlow.

Warwick had two daughters, Isabel and Anne. He married Anne to the son of Henry VI to cement their alliance. The elder daughter, Isabel, was married to Edward and Richard's brother, George, now Duke of Clarence. Whether Warwick intended to eventually place George upon the throne is unclear but Clarence was certainly vain and ambitious. He joined Warwick and rebelled against his brother the King. Richard had grown up with the stories that surrounded Warwick of brave adventure. He had spent many of his formative years in Warwick's household and learned how to be a noble knight from the Earl. Warwick must have sought Richard's support for his uprising too, but Richard refused to give it and remained staunchly loyal to Edward throughout all that followed.

Edward lost his throne for six months from October 1470 to April 1471. On his eighteenth birthday, 2nd October 1470, Richard boarded a ship from the Norfolk coast with his King and fled with him into a second period of uncertain exile, this time in Burgundy. When Edward mustered his response, Richard landed with him and had his first taste of real fighting at the Battle of Barnet. He acquitted himself well in the fog and at the Battle of Tewkesbury that followed was given a command of his own. Warwick died at Barnet and there is no record of Richard's reaction but it seems natural that he would have felt relief at the passing of the greatest enemy of his House whilst also mourning the loss of his mentor and father figure. Henry VI's son was killed at Tewkesbury and with him gone the Lancastrian cause collapsed. Margaret of Anjou was captured and ransomed back to France where she lived the rest of her life in obscurity. Henry VI was disposed of when Edward returned to London. The killing of King Henry is often attributed to Richard personally but, although he was in London, there is no direct evidence to link him with the deed. Even if he had done it personally, it would not doubt have been at the instruction of his brother. The story that Richard killed Henry himself seems to have been woven into the dark reputation he acquired as early proof of a predisposition to such acts. Either way, he would have learned from his brother that a King can tolerate no other King to live should he wish for security.

Lord Of The North

Following Warwick's rebellion, King Edward was left with a problem. A vacuum of power that Warwick had previously inhabited. Edward had come to terms with George and forgiven him, but he could not afford to allow Warwick's estates to fall wholesale into George's hands by virtue of his marriage to Warwick's daughter. That would surely lead to a swift repeat of history.

In 1472, Richard married Warwick's other, widowed daughter, Anne. This match has produced much speculation about Richard and his motives too. Certainly Anne brought with her a hefty inheritance, the other half of Warwick's estates. The match also had advantages for Edward in reducing George's share and therefore his threat. There is a legend that George and Isabel kept Anne under house arrest, working in the kitchens of one of George's retainers to prevent her from remarrying and dividing the inheritance. The story goes that Richard found her and freed her much to George's vexation.

It is also possible, though impossible to prove, that there was at least an element of a love match involved. Richard may well have known Anne a little from his time at Middleham and may have nurtured feelings for her. It is also possible that Richard saw marrying Anne as a way to protect her and repay Warwick for the kindness he had shown the young

Richard in his household. Perhaps he saw a kind of duty to his mentor and that formed a part of his thinking too. This, though, is all speculation. Eyewitness accounts report that Richard and Anne were very close and loved each other, but it is difficult to know what goes on behind closed doors, especially ones closed 500 years ago.

The Warwick estate was eventually divided between George, who took the Midlands and Welsh border areas, and Richard, who acquired all of the northern territories. Warwick's widow was deprived of all of her property and there is some evidence that she went to live at Middleham with Richard and Anne for a time. Richard acquired the northern estates at the expense of Anne's cousin, George Neville. For his protection, Edward made Richard's title to the properties dependent upon the line of male heirs of the body of George Neville. Should George's male line fail, Richard's title to the lands would revert to a lifetime interest only. Interestingly, no such restriction was laid upon the rebellious George. Again, we can only surmise the dismay Richard must have felt at being dealt with in such a manner. Clarence had rebelled yet held full title to his wife's inheritance. Richard had been nothing but loyal, sharing the king's exile and aiding in his retaking of the throne, yet was repaid with restrictions that meant that he relied upon others for his own security.

In spite of this, Richard offered a decade of faultless service to his brother in controlling the notoriously uncontrollable north of England. Richard became immensely popular in the region, championing its causes at court. He sought tax reductions for the region and sought to improve the financial situation he found there. He also took a keen interest in legal matters, showing a concern for the common man that must have seemed outrageous at the time. Two examples offered by A.J. Pollard in Richard III And The Princes In The Tower have long stuck in my mind.

A John Randson appealed to Richard in 1480 against Sir Robert Claxton of Horden, a leading member of the local gentry, who Randson claimed was preventing him from working on his own land. Not only was Claxton of higher social rank, but he was father to one of Richard's retainers and father-in-law to another. These social and family ties would have been expected to see Claxton's cause championed by the Duke. However, Richard found in favour of Randson, warning Claxton 'so to demean you that we have no cause to provide his legal remedy in this behalf'.

Even earlier, in 1473, a petition to Parliament told how Richard had unknowingly taken into service the father of Katherine Williamson of Riccall's husband's murderers. When Richard discovered that the man had aided and abetted his sons he ordered that 'the said Thomas should be brought unto the gaol of York, there to abide, unto the time that he ... were lawfully acquitted or attainted'. At this time, it would have been usual for those wearing the livery of a lord to expect their protection from such a charge, but

Richard was not swayed by such concerns in his pursuit of fair justice for all.

Acts such as these could be construed as ploys on Richard's part to court favour in the north, yet he also risked upsetting the more powerful elements there. Less favourable opinions of him have viewed such things as examples of Richard's dissembling, disingenuous nature in building his reputation in readiness for an assault upon the throne. If this is so, he played a truly long game, for over a decade with no obvious prospect of the Crown and no hint of any attempt to launch a bid surviving. He was not perfect. He dealt harshly with the elderly Countess of Oxford, bullying her into signing over her lands by threatening to house her in one of his icy northern castles, something that she feared would kill her. He could certainly be ruthless in the pursuit of what he wanted.

Militarily, Richard also proved a boon to his adopted region. The Scottish borders had long been lawless with frequent raids into England, often launched from Berwick. Richard held these incursions at bay so that the region felt secure for the first time in living memory and probably beyond it. He led several successful campaigns against the Scottish, the pinnacle of his achievements coming in 1482 when the Scottish King James III threatened to invade. Seizing the initiative from his dithering brother, Richard marched on Berwick, seizing the town unopposed. The citadel of the castle held out. When Richard got word that the Scottish army was marching south, he rode north to meet it. James III was then seized by his own discontented nobles and imprisoned at Edinburgh. His nobles had little stomach for a fight and as Richard burned towns and villages to try and provoke a confrontation, they moved east of the City. Richard entered Edinburgh without the loss of a single man during the campaign. Such was his control of his men that there was no looting and no trouble from the occupying soldiers. He then left Edinburgh unmolested and returned to Berwick where the siege had been won in his absence by Lord Stanley. The campaign was an unmitigated success for England and Berwick has remained an English town from that time to this. Edward IV wrote to the Pope in praise of his brother that 'he alone would suffice to chastise the whole kingdom of Scotland'.

Whatever his motivations, Richard was beloved of York and the north in general as a champion of their long forgotten region. York rejoiced when Richard became King and mourned him after Bosworth, doing all that they could to resist the influence of Henry Tudor without inviting open attack upon the city.

The French Campaign

In 1475, King Edward IV invaded France, seeking to claim the French Crown, long considered the right of English Kings. Henry V had secured a promise that he would inherit the French throne but it had been denied his infant son. Edward was going to take back what had been lost in France and capture that which had eluded all other English monarchs to date. The campaign would bring Edward the martial glory that had made Henry V a legend and would expand his empire abroad. The people would love the glory and the nobility would revel in the spoils of war. Edward's increasingly heavy taxation and extraction of benevolences, forced gifts from wealthy subjects which were hated and resented, were beginning to impinge upon the popularity that his infinitely likeable personality had always afforded him. The French campaign would provide an outlet for this disgruntlement

Charles, Duke of Burgundy was a keen ally. Married to Edward and Richard's sister, Margaret, his territory was under almost constant threat from French desires to consolidate their kingdom, absorbing independent Dukedoms. On 4th July 1475, Edward, Richard and George led a force of around fifteen hundred men at arms and eleven thousand archers as it poured over the Channel to fill Calais. Duke Charles had, for reasons no chronicler seems able to explain, hauled his army east to lay siege to Neuss, part of the Duke of Lorraine's lands. He arrived late to meet Edward and without his army. As Edward marched slowly south, pondering his options, word reached him of the French King's force moving north to meet him.

Edward, despairing of his enigmatic brother-in-law, sought peace. He met King Louis XI at Picquigny, the two monarchs meeting through a wooden barrier on a bridge to avoid any threat of assassination. The Treaty of Picquigny was signed and Edward celebrated it as a success. In return for removing the English army from French soil he received an immediate payment of 75,000 gold crowns with an annual pension of 50,000. Edward's leading advisors received similar payments, which were termed by the English as tributes to make the bribes more palatable. The largest payment went to William, Lord Hastings. The Treaty also provided for the marriage of the French heir to Edward's eldest daughter, Elizabeth. The king, his nobles and their army returned to England untested and far from bathed in glory.

During this episode we have another interesting glimpse of Richard's personality. When Edward called his nobles together to discuss his options, the Dukes of Clarence, Suffolk and Norfolk, the Earls Rivers, Northumberland and Pembroke, the Marquis of Dorset, Lord Hastings, Lord Stanley and many others agreed with the King's desire to seek a favourable peace with Louis. Richard, Duke of Gloucester, dissented. He measured the situation and argued that the English force could easily defeat the French army.

Then the King would have his glory and, if he still wished to seek peace, could negotiate it from a position of strength. It seems likely that Richard's assessment of the English force's chances was correct. They probably could have won. Edward sought peace anyway, but there was no resentment apparent from his brother that his council had been overruled.

When it came time for the Treaty of Picquigny, Richard refused to be a party to it. He returned the French bribe and did not attend. In its time, such a snub was significant and did not go unnoticed. Louis XI earned his nickname of 'The Universal Spider' because of the diplomatic webs that he spun and he knew his enemies well. Edward probably had no real desire for war and was short of money, so Louis bribed him to leave. When the English army arrived to camp at Amiens, Louis laid on so much food and wine that there was no trouble from the English troops in the town. Anyone who opposed the treaty was wooed by Louis. For example, one of Edward's captains was bribed with a thousand crowns for criticising the capitulation. What price would the Spider King pay, then, to appease the royal brother of England's King? Richard did accept an invitation to dine with the French King and received a gift of plate and fine horses, but Louis apparently found Richard a rigid character upon whom he had been unable to make an impression. No doubt he marked the King's martial brother as one to be wary of, a fact that was to haunt Richard later.

Lord Protector

On 9th April 1483, King Edward IV died following a brief illness at the age of forty. He is still the tallest monarch in English history at 6' 4" but his appetite for food and women was legendary (as was that of his grandson, Henry VIII). He had grown portly and lethargic, his taxes and benevolences making him increasingly unpopular in the country. The queen's family, the Woodvilles, were a source of consternation to the nobility. They were a large family and Edward had poured lands and titles upon them to the exclusion of the established nobility so that they were unpopular and resented, considered undeserving upstarts. The queen had children from her first marriage and furnished the king with many more, including two sons. The eldest, Edward, now King Edward V was 12 years of age. His brother, Richard, Duke of York was 9. Young Edward had been installed at Ludlow Castle as Prince of Wales with his own household under the direction of Anthony Woodville, Earl Rivers, brother of the queen. Woodvilles dominated Edward's household and whilst this may appear somewhat natural as his mother's family, it was to prove a significant issue for the young king.

In mid April, Richard was advised by Lord Hastings, a close friend and advisor to Edward IV, that the King was dead and that the queen intended to seize power. Hastings told the Duke that Edward had named him Protector of the Realm during his son's minority but that the queen intended to ignore this provision and exclude the Duke. Richard must have been concerned that he was not advised officially of his own brother's death and his suspicions must have been roused immediately. He wrote to Earl Rivers at Ludlow to arrange to meet the new King's party at Nottingham so that they might enter London together. He also wrote to Henry Stafford, Duke of Buckingham to ask him to accompany them. Henry was the grandson of the Duke into whose care Richard had been placed after Ludlow and it is possible that the memories of the honourable old Duke influenced him in seeking out Henry. Richard held a solemn funeral service for his brother at York on 21st April at which he led the pledges of fealty to the new King Edward V. Richard left York on 23rd April and Edward left Ludlow on 24th. At some point in his journey Richard received a letter from Rivers altering their meeting to Northampton on 29th April. This must have felt even more suspicious atop everything else. Rivers and the new King arrived at Northampton on 29th but whilst Rivers stayed there to await the Protector, the King and the rest of his retinue rode further on to Stoney Stratford, a Woodville manor. When Richard reached Northampton to find the King missing, his concern surely grew. Though Rivers protested that it meant nothing, Richard had him arrested the following morning and rode to Stoney Stratford where he took the King into his custody.

On 1st May, the queen took Edward's brother and other members of her family into sanctuary at Westminster. On the 4th May, Edward entered London with Richard and Buckingham to a rapturous reception as Richard hailed the new King to his people. On 10th May council met and Richard was officially installed as Protector. The council seems to have been impressed with Richard's bloodless seizure of the King from the clutches of the Woodvilles. Coins began to be minted in the name of Edward V whose coronation was set for 22nd June. After his father's death, council had previously intended the coronation to take place on 4th May. This delay has been cited by some as testament to Richard's intention to seize the throne, but following events at Stoney Stratford Edward had not arrived in London until this date. It is also possible that the queen had intended Rivers to rush Edward to London to be crowned and proclaimed of age to rule to preclude Gloucester as Protector by rendering the position unnecessary.

News also reached Richard in London of the death without heir of George Neville. His brother's caution was in danger of back firing on his son. The majority of Richard's land and title reverted to life interests, meaning he had none of it to leave to his precious only son, Edward of Middleham. This was another factor that must have weighed heavy on Richard's mind as he fought the Woodvilles for control of the King. As Protector, he could correct the problem in

Parliament. If he lost his position, he would lose everything and the Woodvilles would win it all.

The Duke of Buckingham was made Constable of England and given effective sovereign power in Wales as a reward for his support. Richard sought to have Rivers and others seized at Stoney Stratford tried for treason but council resisted. Richard installed Edward in the Tower of London, not as a prisoner but using the Royal Apartments there. The Tower was at this time a royal palace like any other. It had a gaol, like other palaces, but it did not gain its bloody reputation until Tudor times. It is therefore hard to read too much into this in itself. Richard also sought to have Edward's brother released from sanctuary to join him. In early June he was taken from sanctuary and placed in the Tower with his brother.

On 13th June Richard called Lord Hastings, Buckingham, Bishop Morton, Bishop Rotherham, Lord Stanley and John Howard to the Tower for a council meeting. Richard left the meeting, returned and cried treason. Hastings was removed and possibly executed immediately. There is some debate about the precise date of the execution, but nonetheless Richard had removed one of Edward IV and Edward V's key supporters at court on little evidence. We see here a ruthless streak and a determination to act decisively that contributes to the suspicion beginning to surround Richard even at this point. Stanley, Morton and Rotherham were arrested but later released.

Richard appeared to have gained complete control, installing close friends such as Lord Lovell alongside

Buckingham to support him and excluding the Woodvilles. Hastings was lambasted as the prime encourager of Edward IV's debauchery. Preparations continued for Edward's coronation. Richard was secure as Lord Protector.

Bad Blood

It is hard to pinpoint the precise moment that Richard decided to take the throne from his nephew. Had he arrived in London so wary of the influence of the Woodvilles on the new King that it already occurred to him? Was this the opportunity that he had awaited so patiently for over a decade? Did he seize Edward at Stoney Stratford with the intention of stealing his throne? Had Buckingham been whispering in his ear? It is hard to distinguish. Certainly Richard had an armed force despatched from York in case he required it. He took control of the boy, swept the Woodvilles aside and removed the loyal support of Lord Hastings. This can be viewed as paving the way for a usurpation, but it could also be simply decisive action to secure the safety of the realm as was his role as Protector. Nothing survives to conclusively answer this question.

As a Ricardian, I am bound to view Richard's previous exemplary behaviour and unswerving loyalty, his commitment to justice and duty and see a man reacting to the events that he found. It must also be accepted that it is every bit as possible that he intended to take the throne even before he left York, that the chance he had been waiting for had arrived. There is no evidence of this man before 1483, yet he certainly emerges during that summer.

The basis upon which Richard took the throne is well worth an examination since it will differentiate between a usurper seizing an opportunity and a reluctant man doing his duty. Probably in early June, Bishop Stillington approached the Protector with a matter of grave concern. The story that he imparted changed the course of English history. The Bishop claimed to have been party to a pre-contract of marriage between King Edward IV and Lady Eleanor Butler before the King had married Elizabeth Woodville.

A pre-contract to marry in mediaeval terms equated to an actual marriage as if there had been a wedding ceremony. It could be created as simply as saying 'I will marry you' but was binding in the eyes of Church, State and God. Lady Eleanor Butler had passed away by 1483 but crucially was still alive when Edward married Elizabeth Woodville. This meant that Edward was already effectively married and so his marriage to Elizabeth was bigamous. The effect of this was that any children of that marriage were illegitimate and unable to inherit the Crown.

In mediaeval legal terms this was an absolute. There was no way around it. If true, it meant that Edward V and his brother were illegitimate and unable to take the throne. George had been executed some years earlier when Edward IV had lost patience with his constant plotting. Therefore the only legitimate male heir of the House of York was Richard, Duke of Gloucester. Legally, he was King. He had two options. He could suppress the information and allow the Coronation Ceremony to correct any fault in young Edward's title or he could become king himself. The decision was made in the instant he made the pre-contract public. Again, the interpretation of this action is the chasing of an elusive truth. Did Richard relish the opportunity? Who would not wish to be King? Viewed in terms of his duty, Church law meant that he should be King. Temporal law made him the only rightful King. His duty was clearly to take the throne whether he wanted to or not.

The existence of the Butler pre-contract is disputed but in his book Eleanor The Secret Queen, John Ashdown-Hill makes a powerful case for its existence. Once more, though, it must be acknowledged that there is a possibility that it was fabricated to facilitate Richard's thrust for power.

It is also suggested by several sources that Richard considered questioning the legitimacy of his brother too, but later refrained from pursuing it, perhaps not seeing the need to dishonour his mother. King Louis XI of France had long joked, fairly openly, that Edward IV was the son of an English archer named Bleybourne. He called the English King Edward Bleybourne to much amusement in France. But was there more to this than the old enmity?

Edward had been born on 28th April 1442 in Rouen, Normandy. His father, the Duke of York, was fighting the English cause in France at the time and reports state that he left on campaign around eleven months before Edward's birth. These dates are preserved in the records of Rouen Cathedral and clearly the maths does not add up. In addition, Edward was christened in a quiet ceremony in a side chapel of the Cathedral on the Duke's return. This is unusually restrained for the first born son of the greatest noble in the land. Unless, of course, the Duke knew that Edward was not, in fact, his first born son. In contrast, Edmund's birth the following year was celebrated lavishly with a christening in the full Cathedral. Edmund was the son who the Duke kept close throughout the conflicts of the Wars of the Roses. Possibly he intended at some point to name Edmund his heir, but he never did. Both died together at Wakefield and Edward went on to take the throne. The christening evidence is somewhat circumstantial but the evidence of the dates of Edward's birth is not. Precluding some carnal rush back from the front, the Duke of York cannot have been Edward's father. However, the Duke never marked Edward as illegitimate, nor did he ever treat him as anything other than his rightful heir. A hasty christening may also be a red herring as the Duke and Duchess had already lost children in infancy and baptism was considered essential for passage into Heaven. This matter is therefore, as yet, unproven, but rumour of it did exist at the time.

This fact, added to Edward's pre-contract, made Edward V doubly illegitimate and perhaps made up Richard's mind for him. Bishop Stillington had been close to George, Duke of Clarence and it is possible that Richard began to wonder whether his brother's unrelenting rebellions were due to the fact that he knew this information and believed himself the rightful king.

If Richard created both of these sets of evidence then he went to great lengths to discredit the brother he had served loyally for all of his adult life, against whom he had refused to rebel. He also dishonoured his mother and made his father a cuckold. This lack of family loyalty seems uncharacteristic, yet perhaps events at Ludlow all that time ago played upon the Duke's mind. His father had abandoned him to his fate there. So had his eldest brother. If it was revenge, he had waited coldly for over twenty years to exact it. Or perhaps it just made accepting the truth a little easier. If it was true, he may also have felt betrayed by his entire family.

The Church and Parliament asked Richard to take the throne as the only legal, rightful heir and he was crowned King Richard III on 6th July 1483 at the age of 30. As his scoliosis worsened and perhaps became more and more painful, the fact that he was God's anointed King of England must have offered some comfort to Richard. He may have felt himself justified, forgiven of whatever he feared had caused him to be afflicted.

Buckingham's Rebellion

Richard was crowned King Richard III with all of the pomp and ceremony required. All of the Lords Spiritual and Temporal that could be there were in attendance. There was an attempt at some reconciliation. A Woodville bishop was amongst the congregation and Lord Stanley was appointed to Richard's household. The King and his Queen set off on a grand progress around the country. Contemporary sources state frequently how well he was received at every stop. Subjects offered him coin only to be told by the King that he did not want their money, only their love. The country seemed to want him and to be looking forward to his rule.

On 8th September the King was in York and had his 9 year old son invested as Prince of Wales. It has been suggested that the investiture was a rushed affair and that it plays a part in the mystery of the fate of the sons of Edward IV, but it is equally possible that Richard planned to have the ceremony in the city that was so close to his heart, and to honour the city that loved him so now that he was not just their lord but their King. Shortly after this, though, trouble erupted from several unlikely sources.

The first sign of trouble was a march on London by men of Kent on 10th October. The Duke of Norfolk dealt swiftly with the uprising. He captured and interrogated the leaders and reported the disturbing news that he uncovered to Richard. In late September, the Duke of Buckingham, effectively Richard's right-hand-man, had written to some exile by the name of Henry Tudor encouraging him to invade. Buckingham was to lead a force out of Wales, Tudor was to land on the south coast and Kent was to rise and march on London. All of this was planned for 18th October. Kent acted eight days too early and alerted the authorities to the plot.

As the date of the uprising approached, England was ravaged by violent rain storms. Tudor left Brittany on 2nd October, backed by Duke Francis of Brittany to the tune of 10,000 crowns and 5,000 mercenaries. He also may have had a portion of Edward IV's treasury, stolen by Elizabeth Woodville's brother, suggesting a Woodville backing of the plot. Buckingham's force began to move out of Wales but found no way across the swollen torrent of the River Severn. In the foul weather, the Duke's army began to disband and head home. The Duke himself fled into hiding.

On 1st November, Henry Stafford, Duke of Buckingham was captured and delivered to King Richard at Salisbury. Buckingham had been hiding with a sympathiser in Shropshire whose sympathy evaporated when Richard put a substantial price on the Duke's head. It was said that before he was captured, Buckingham had his infant son smuggled away dressed as a girl. This son, Edward Stafford, was to be restored under the Tudors only to fall victim to Henry VIII's vicious suspicion in 1521. Richard refused Buckingham's pleas to see him. Edward Stafford would later claim that his father had intended to stab Richard with a hidden knife, but Richard refused to give him an audience and ordered his execution the following day.

That very day, the remnants of Tudor's fleet, battered by the same storms that had hindered Buckingham, reached the south coast. A small group of soldiers waved them ashore, hailing the success of the rebellion. Henry, narrowing his eyes no doubt with a shrewdness that was to become his trademark, did not believe the news and turned the bedraggled fleet back toward Brittany.

This glimpse of Richard is less telling than the fact of the rebellion itself. To call it Buckingham's Rebellion is something of a misnomer. The Duke appears to have been recruited to the plot rather than the instigator, possibly by Bishop Morton who was his prisoner at Brecknock following the incident at council that had seen Hastings executed. Doubtless the betrayal cut Richard deeply. He was a man of honour and found such dishonourable behaviour abhorrent. Richard wrote to his Chancellor, John Russell, Bishop of Lincoln before Buckingham's capture and added a postscript in his own hand, stating 'Here, loved be God, all is well and truly determined for to resist the malice of him that had best cause to be true, the duke of Buckingham, the most untrue creature living, whom, with God's grace, we shall not be long till that we will be in that parts and subdue his malice. We assure you there never was falser traitor purveyed for...'. The outraged disgust pours from the page.

Buckingham had pledged himself to Richard and had been amply rewarded, so why did he join this rebellion? The answer is not definitively known. It has been suggested by Virgil, a chronicler writing 30 years later, that the Duke had not been given part of an inheritance Edward IV had withheld and Richard had promised him. This award was in fact made and only awaiting Parliamentary approval. Another possibility is that Buckingham saw a chance to seize the throne for himself. He was a cousin to Richard and had royal blood. He was also vain and ambitious, much as Richard's brother George had been. As with George, Richard appears not to have equated these personality traits with a proclivity for rebellion. Perhaps Buckingham saw Tudor as no real threat, raised a large force of his own and aimed to grasp power himself in the confusion.

The stated aim of the rebellion began as securing the release of Edward V and returning him to the throne. This was swiftly redirected though to placing Henry Tudor on the throne. It has been suggested that Buckingham had the boys killed in the Tower to remove them, believing Tudor would secure no support in the country and his own road to power would be left wide open. An opposing hypothesis is that Buckingham learned of the boy's murder at Richard's hands and was so outraged that he joined the planned uprising, informing, them of the deed so that Tudor became the figurehead.

Whatever the true reasons, the rebellion may well have left Richard stronger rather than undermined. His enemies had exposed themselves as traitors for all to see. Buckingham was the only noble to revolt. The remainder who joined were former loyalists of Edward IV and the Woodvilles along with the exiled remnants of the Lancastrian party. Luck had certainly played a part, as Kent misfired its assault on London and storms prevented Richard's enemies from making good their plans. The King had also acted with his trademark decisiveness in crushing the rebels and disposing of the treacherous Buckingham, the ruthless streak that had cut short Lord Hastings' life surfacing one more. Yet what less should be expected of a mediaeval king?

The north and midlands remained staunchly loyal to the King, only the south offering opposition. His greatest ally had exposed himself as false and been dealt with. All that remained was to root out the dregs of Lancastrian resistance and Edwardian loyalty that had found a focus in Henry Tudor.

Not A Drop Of Doubtful Royal Blood

It is worth examining Henry Tudor a little closer at this point as it makes clear just how close Richard was to eliminating any source of opposition to his rule. Henry Tudor emerged as the last and final Lancastrian hope. On Christmas Day 1483, he stood in Rouen Cathedral and pledged to marry Elizabeth of York, daughter of Edward IV, upon becoming King of England. In so doing, he galvanised Edwardian sympathy and the Woodville faction to his own Lancastrian support and presented the last real threat that Richard needed to face.

Henry Tudor's claim to the throne was, at best, flimsy. In reality, it was non-existent. His parents had married when his mother was 12 and his father 24. His father was Edmund Tudor, maternal half brother to King Henry VI. He died of the plague in captivity before Henry's birth. Edmund Tudor's mother was Henry V's widow, Catherine of Valois, a French Princess. This meant that he possessed French royal blood, but Salic Law in France prevented female succession.

Henry's mother was Lady Margaret Beaufort. She gave birth to Henry at the age of thirteen on a stormy night at Pembroke Castle. The birth was difficult and was perhaps the reason that, despite subsequent marriages, Margaret never had another child. Henry, then, was her pride and joy. Lady Margaret was descended from John of Gaunt, Duke of Lancaster and father to King Henry IV. However, the Beauforts were children John shared with a mistress, Katherine Swynford. When John eventually married Katherine Richard II agreed to legitimise their children in Parliament on the condition that the line was specifically barred from royal succession. Henry, then, had no claim to the throne of England.

Caught upon the wrong side of the Wars of the Roses, Henry was eventually forced into exile in Brittany with his uncle Jasper Tudor at fourteen. His mother remained in England and the separation was no doubt painful to them both. By 1483, Lady Margaret was married to Lord Stanley, an immensely powerful baron owning swathes of the north west and able to call upon a vast force of men at arms. It is perhaps Margaret who saw, or created, the opportunity for her son. She held him up as the last Lancastrian, the last alternative to Ricardian rule. She negotiated with Elizabeth Woodville in sanctuary for the marriage of their children to unite the Houses of York and Lancaster behind her son.

Buckingham's Rebellion began with the intention of freeing the Princes in the Tower but quickly changed its aim to placing Henry Tudor on the throne. If the fate of the Princes became known to Elizabeth Woodville, it is possible Margaret Beaufort told her to galvanise Woodville backing. It is even possible that she told Elizabeth of their fate without actually knowing it, banking on the lack of information that would be reaching the former queen.

Henry evaded Richard in 1483 and returned to Brittany. Richard opened negotiations during 1484 to have Henry handed over in return for the supply of English archers to assist Brittany in fending off France. Word of the plan reached Tudor and he managed to slip away over the French border. The French court, under Louis XI's son Charles VIII, welcomed Tudor. The French possibly remembered Richard's burning desire for battle on French soil and saw Tudor as a welcome alternative, or at least a diversion. Henry set up a faux court and die hard Lancastrians and disaffected Yorkists flocked to him. When the captain of the Calais garrison defected, he took with him John de Vere, 13th Earl of Oxford who had been his prisoner. The Earl was the most experienced Lancastrian military commander alive, a formidable opponent. The sheep now had a tame wolf in their midst. The unthinkable was becoming inevitable.

Parliament

King Richard III held only one Parliament, in 1484. His legislative programme is fascinating because of the promise that it held and also the problems it could create. It is possible to view Richard as an early social reformer. He championed the cause of the common people during his time in the north and did not shy away from trampling on the ancient rights of the nobility either. To do this on a national scale, though, was a whole different matter. The nobility of England had a vested interest in the status quo. It kept them rich, powerful and comfortable. They were unlikely to welcome any rocking of the steady ship of feudal England. Perhaps Richard saw in this structure the cause of civil conflict and strife. Maybe he sought to sow the seeds of change, but if he did, he would have a battle on his hands.

The first striking thing about Richard's Parliament is that its Acts were published in English. The law in England had always been the preserve of the wealthy and educated, the Church and the nobility who could read Latin. Richard published his laws in English so that all may have access to them. Accepting that literacy was not yet high, this still opened access and understanding of the law to the common man. Their law was in their language. It must have felt more like their law, their possession, than it ever had before. With this gift to the commoners came a removal of a long guarded privilege of the nobility and Church and they were likely to resent it.

Parliament passed 33 statutes in total. Titulus Regius detailed Richard claim to the throne. It formally declared the children of Edward IV and Elizabeth Woodville illegitimate and identified Richard's son, Edward of Middleham, Prince of Wales as his heir. Other private acts attainted those involved in the rebellion for treason, settled some inheritance claims and provided benefits for individuals.

Benevolences, which Edward IV had used widely and successfully but which were deeply unpopular, were abolished. The Act stated that 'The subjects of this realm shall not be charged with any benevolences'. This was popular within the nobility and within the merchant class, who felt more able to invest their money in growth without the threat of being forced to provide a gift to the Crown. It was also viewed as a statement of Richard's intent to manage Crown finances responsibly so that he would not need to resort to benevolences.

Richard's Parliament made several reforms to the judicial system to deal with corruption, including the prevalent bribing of juries. The system of bail was extended and reinforced to prevent a person from being imprisoned before trial and protect their goods from seizure before they were found guilty. A malicious, false charge could previously see a man in jail with all of his goods seized. Even if he was found innocent, his goods did not have to be returned to him. Richard's Parliament corrected the injustices the

King saw here, perhaps before his ducal courts whilst in the north.

Further Acts protected English merchants and tradesmen from foreign competition to the delight of London in particular and sought to abolish the widespread fraud in transactions of land. The wool trade was also freed from abuse that had hounded it. One area that was protected, even from the anti-alien legislation, was the flourishing printing and book industries. Parliament ensured that this burgeoning trade in learning was preserved and books flowed out of London as well as in from the Continent.

It is impossible to know how far Richard may have taken his reforms given time, but it is striking the instant impact that he sought to make in his first Parliament. It is argued that the Acts of Richard's Parliament cannot be wholly attributed to him as the machinery of government existed to deal with these matters, but this was still very much a time of personal monarchy when the King ruled as well as reigned. In addition, we can see much of Richard's ideas and ideals from his time in the north translating to the national stage.

When Cardinal Wolsey attempted to extract benevolences from Londoners on behalf of Henry VIII forty years later, the mayor and aldermen of London confidently referenced Richard's statute outlawing them which had never been repealed. When Wolsey berated them for quoting the laws of a usurper and murderer, the men supposedly replied 'Although he did evil, yet in his time were many good Acts made'.

Sir Francis Bacon, Lord Chancellor to King James I and a respected Parliamentarian later described Richard III as 'A good lawmaker for the ease and solace of the common people'. It seems that the one thing even Richard's detractors agree upon is that he was a maker of good laws for the benefit of his people.

Personal Disasters

Around the end of March or beginning of April 1484, the precise date is uncertain, Richard's world began to fall apart. His beloved son died suddenly at Middleham in Yorkshire at the age of ten. Richard and his wife Anne had only one child, upon whom Richard had doubtless built his hopes in the north, for whom he had gathered a substantial inheritance whilst in the north and who had been his heir apparent, the Prince of Wales. The couple were reportedly distraught. Aside from the personal tragedy, this created a dynastic issue for Richard. He could not afford the insecurity of having no heir and so must name someone. Two candidates emerged. The son of his brother, George, Duke of Clarence was nine years old. A child heir would bring with it well known problems. When it was his own son, it was one matter, but could he choose a child now? Edward, Earl of Warwick was the last remaining male heir of the House of York, so his claim was strong, but Richard eventually named another nephew, John de la Pole, Earl of Lincoln.

John was the eldest son of Richard's sister Elizabeth and her husband the Duke of Suffolk. At around twenty, he was a man, though his claim may have been considered slightly weaker as it was through the female line. Salic Law did not rule in England, but succession through a male line was still generally preferred. The Earl of Lincoln was placed in control of the Council of the North as Richard had been and he proved capable in the role.

It is unclear whether Richard may have intended to name Warwick his heir when he came of age. He placed the young boy and his sister into the care of Lincoln's household to be educated. Lincoln may have been aware that he was a stop gap heir, or Richard may have fully intended to groom Lincoln for power.

Richard was, at this time, only 31 years old and there was a chance that he could still have more children and a male heir of his own. He is known to have had two illegitimate children, probably from before his marriage to Anne. It is notable that Richard, celebrated for his pious devotion, is not known to have had any mistresses during his marriage. As King, he publically berated the immorality of his brother and his court. He provided well for his two illegitimate children, but having disinherited his illegitimate nephews, neither his son nor daughter could have been candidates for the throne. Later, Henry VIII considered legitimising his only illegitimate son to make him heir, but Richard does not appear to have seriously entertained this as an option.

Further tragedy struck in March of 1485 when Anne succumbed to tuberculosis. The illness had killed her sister Isabel and now claimed her life too. An infection in the lungs, the disease causes a persistent cough, blood filled sputum and would have cause Anne's body to waste. It was incurable and unstoppable, even with the medical knowledge at the King's disposal. He had lost his precious son and now his beloved wife of thirteen years was following. Richard surely felt that his world was falling apart around him. He is recorded as weeping openly at her funeral at Westminster Abbey.

To add insult to injury, a rumour sprang up, possibly created by Tudor's growing faction, perhaps even by his mother Lady Margaret, that Richard had been poisoning his wife so that, with her dead, he could marry his own niece, Elizabeth, in order to prevent Tudor from doing so. There is certainly no surviving evidence that this was the case but such was the concern that two of Richard closest advisors, Sir Richard Ratcliffe and Sir William Catesby told him that he must deny the rumours publically. Anne's Neville family in the north could easily become dangerously disaffected if they were to believe the rumours. Eventually Richard agreed to release a denial that he intended to marry his niece, though remained silent on the question of his wife's poisoning. Perhaps he did not wish to dignify the allegation with an answer, but his silence about this, as about other issues, did not necessarily do him any good.

When Henry Tudor's long expected invasion finally came in August of 1485, Richard may have had nothing left to lose.

The Battle of Bosworth Field

On 22nd August 1485, Richard III's army faced off against Henry Tudor's collection of rebels and mercenaries. It is likely that most viewed the outcome as a certain victory for the King. He had never yet been defeated in battle whereas Tudor was untried. Richard had with him the Duke of Norfolk and his son along with the Earl of Northumberland, Henry Percy. Richard also took the field with a host of his loyal friends, including Francis Lovell, Richard Ratcliffe, James Harrington and many others. These were close personal friends to the king, most having been drawn to his good lordship in the north and his valour on the battlefield. Richard was not one for the tournament as his brother had been, but was more than prepared for the real thing. These men loved him and would literally lay down their lives for him.

Henry Tudor had landed at Milford Haven in Wales on Sunday 7th August. He had brought with him around 2,000 men, mostly mercenaries supplied by France, and moved through Wales swelling his numbers, though perhaps not by the amount he had hoped. The betrayal of King Richard began almost immediately. Milford Haven was under the jurisdiction of Rhys ap Thomas who Richard had promoted to Principal Lieutenant in south west Wales. Thomas had offered a vow to his King to show his fealty that: 'Whoever ill-fated to the state, shall dare to land in these parts of Wales where I have employment under your majesty, must resolve with himself to make his entrance and irruption over my belly'. Thomas did not resist Tudor, but joined his forces. In order to sooth his honour without being embarrassed in front of his men, Thomas stood below a bridge as Tudor passed over it. Thus Henry Tudor had made his entrance over Thomas's belly, though it was hardly in the spirit of his oath.

By the time he reached Bosworth, Tudor had around 5,000 men. The King had a force of 6,000. The Earl of Northumberland brought a further 3,000 and Lord Stanley fielded his own huge force of 4,000 men. Stanley was supposed to take the field for the king but had a long reputation of sitting on the sidelines until the outcome was decided, or until he could decide it and take the glory for the victory. He had built a private empire based upon this cautious, watchful approach. He was also, by virtue of his marriage, step-father to Henry Tudor who had courted his support since landing. Characteristically, Stanley had not openly committed to either side. Richard was sufficiently suspicious to hold Stanley's son, Lord Strange, a hostage for his father's good behaviour. With his larger force of fiercely loyal men, Richard should have been confident of victory against the rabble assembled before him.

The Duke of Norfolk led Richard's forces into battle. It is uncharacteristic of Richard to sit back. He had placed the Crown upon his helm, something Henry V had done at Agincourt, yet he held back.

Perhaps, pragmatically, he did not wish to risk his life with his succession insecure. It is also possible that by this time his scoliosis was increasingly painful and restrictive. The Earl of Oxford led Tudor's vanguard and the fighting was fierce and close, but the Duke of Norfolk was killed and the Earl of Oxford pressed forward. Richard ordered the Earl of Northumberland to engage but he did not move. He ordered Lord Stanley into the fray and he remained still. Richard apparently gave the order for Lord Strange's execution for his father's betrayal, though the order was never followed through.

It was at this point, as the battle was turning against him, that Richard spotted a small group breaking away from the rear of Tudor's army. The invader's banner was flying with them and they were making for Lord Stanley's position to Richard's right, no doubt to personally implore Tudor's step-father to intervene. Richard spotted an opportunity to end things once and for all, one way or another. With his close knit band of brothers in arms, he lowered his lance and spurred his destrier toward the small group. It must have been a sight to behold as the King and his mounted knights thundered down the hill and closed upon the enemy in a blaze of colour and a flash of gleaming plate armour. When it became clear that the approaching charge would reach them before they reached Lord Stanley, Tudor and his retinue turned to face the oncoming attack.

The two forces clashed in a microcosm of the main battle. One by one, Richard friends fell as they ploughed closer to Henry. Ratcliffe, Harrington and all of the others were cut down, but Richard got within feet of Tudor. He personally killed Tudor's standard bearer William Brandon, a measure of how close he came and he slew Sir John Cheney, a giant of a man and at least as experienced a soldier as Richard. Contrary to the popular myth, sources state that Richard was offered a horse by a squire and encouraged to flee the battlefield. Richard refused, telling them he would leave the field as undisputed King of England, or not at all. Perhaps his own abandonment at Ludlow all of those years before had left a deep mark. He would not do the same to his men or his kingdom.

Now, Lord Stanley saw his opportunity. Richard was isolated and failing. He ordered his brother Sir William to attack the King. Richard fell and was killed. Polydore Virgil, who wrote his Historiae Anglicae for Henry Tudor some twenty year later, conceded that 'King Richard alone was killed fighting manfully in the thickest press of his enemies'. Much like his lawmaking, even his enemies could not bring themselves to criticise his bravery and prowess on the field of battle. The discovery of the scoliosis exhibited by his skeleton makes this martial strength all the more impressive for the restricting pain that it must have caused to the very end.

The legend states that Lord Stanley found the Crown that had fallen from Richard's head and placed it upon that of his step-son. So began the Tudor dynasty. The Plantagenets had ruled England for over three hundred years. They remain the longest ruling dynasty in English history. Richard was also the last King of England to die in battle. His death ushered in the Tudor age and all that it brought to England, for good or ill. It also sealed his fate as a figure of evil in English history.

Hornby Castle - The Price of Power

Treachery at Bosworth has long been cried, since King Richard was not supported by men he legitimately expected to fight for him. Foremost amongst this shadowy clique was Thomas, Lord Stanley. The reason for Lord Stanley's betrayal of his king is perhaps not hard to fathom; he was step-father to Henry Tudor and so had a right to expect a great deal of power in compensation for his actions, or rather, lack of actions.

Yet there is more to this story. Stretching back over two decades lies a dispute in which Richard, as Duke of Gloucester and then as king, took sides. Perhaps even more than becoming step-father to a king, this matter may have played on Lord Stanley's mind as he watched from the sidelines as the two armies prepared to fight to the death for the Crown of England. No doubt he also enjoyed being courted by both parties.

The dispute in question was between the Stanley family and the Harrington family. Both were gentry families in the north west, with the Stanley's increasing their wealth and influence under Thomas's grandfather, Sir John, and father, Sir Thomas, the first Baron Stanley. By the mid 15th century they owned great swathes of north west England and held many offices of power in the region. During the Wars of the Roses, Lord Stanley developed a reputation for staying out of battles until the result was clear and then joining, usually by sending his younger brother Sir William's forces into the fray, on the winning side, thus reaping the rewards of seeming to decide the battle. He fought variously for Lancaster and York and just as often failed to arrive at battles. Thus the Stanley's position had been won carefully, by ensuring that whether York or Lancaster prevailed, the Stanleys always stood to gain. For these reasons Lord Stanley is often seen as a fickle, conniving, self-serving man. If one were to seek to give him the benefit of the doubt, we may allow that he headed a family on the cusp of real greatness after several generations of hard work. One wrong move at this time could cost the entire family everything that they had. Perhaps he did not feel willing or able to take that risk.

The Harrington family are perhaps the very antithesis of the Stanleys. James Harrington was a friend and supporter of Richard as Lord of the North. His grandfather had carried Henry V's banner at the battle of Agincourt where Richard's great uncle had been slain. The two men were soaked in the chivalric memories of English glory on French soil. Throughout the Wars of the Roses, the Harringtons fought for York and never wavered. Sir James is one of the candidates for having carried Richard's banner at Bosworth, a fitting repeat of Agincourt as the king led a charge of his cavalry across the shuddering field. Certainly, Sir James died at the king's side that day.

The beginnings of the Stanley feud with the Harringtons lie at the Battle of Wakefield on 30th

December 1460. Not because they fought on opposing sides; Stanley managed to miss this battle. Richard's father, the Duke of York and brother Edmund, Earl of Rutland were killed when the Yorkist army was destroyed. Also killed was James's father Thomas and James's eldest brother John. Initial reports stated that Thomas died in the fighting and John of his wounds shortly after the battle. This meant that Thomas Harrington's possessions passed on his death to John and on John's death to his heirs. Anne and Elizabeth Harrington were about four and five years old and the law stated that the inheritance would pass to whoever they married.

James Harrington and his brother Robert argued that John had in fact died before Thomas, making James the rightful heir. Lord Stanley immediately set about making the two girls his wards and marrying them to his son and nephew. The jewel in the Harrington family crown was Hornby Castle. A stunning property, it sat above the valley of the River Lune, firmly in Stanley country. Obtaining it would allow them to join territories together and thoroughly dominate the area.

Edward IV, measuring Stanley's might, feared upsetting him and granted him control of the Harrington girls and therefore possession of Hornby. James Harrington, who had been amongst those who captured Henry VI in 1465 and delivered him to Edward, must have felt somewhat betrayed after his loyal service. Anyway, he and his brother refused to surrender their nieces or the castle and dug their heels in behind the mighty walls of Hornby.

When the Earl of Warwick rebelled, Stanley seized the opportunity to try and drive the Harringtons out for good. He brought up a giant cannon named 'Mile Ende' from Bristol with the intention of blasting the troublesome Harringtons out of Hornby. Not a shot was fired however, and it is intriguing to find a warrant issued by Richard on 26th March 1470, signed 'at Hornby'. The seventeen year old Duke had chosen his side, and it was the loyal Harringtons that he backed, perhaps perceiving an injustice they suffered at his brother's hands that their service did not merit, in contrast to Stanley. In Richard, the north found 'good lordship' to check the advance of Stanley power. Lord Stanley found himself blocked by the king's own brother.

In 1483, when Richard became king, evidence suggests that he intended to re-open the issue of ownership of Hornby, no doubt to the joy of the loyal Sir James, but to the dismay and disgust of Lord Stanley, whose son and daughter-in-law now lived at the castle. Add to this the appointments of Richard Ratcliffe, the new king's friend and uncle of Robert Harrington's wife, as king's deputy in the West Marches and Sherriff of Westmorland, Robert's brother-in-law John Pilkington as Steward of Rochdale and Richard III's chamberlain and another Harrington family member, John Huddlestone, as Warden of the West Marches, Sheriff of Cumberland and Steward of

Penrith and we see Stanley influence being strangled in the region.

No doubt this restriction of Lord Stanley's expansionism was intentional on Richard's part, but as Thomas Stanley surveyed Bosworth Field, this must have been playing on his mind. Should he maintain upon the throne the man who was seeking to destroy him, or replace him with a step-son full of gratitude with power to dispense accordingly? Richard III had appointed Stanley Steward of his Household and made him a Knight of the Garter, perhaps not entirely able to escape his brother's recognition of Stanley as a necessary evil given the huge force of armed men that he was able to call upon. But was this enough to compensate Stanley for the dismantling of his north western empire, or did he see an opportunity for more? Henry VII made him Earl of Derby, a title his family still hold today. Measured dispassionately, it was a good decision that has made the family in a way Thomas's father and grandfather could only have dreamed of. The Harringtons, for all of their unswerving loyalty, were wiped out, destroyed, along with the House of York they had fought alongside for so long.

In this respect, Lord Stanley's betrayal of his king at Bosworth appears foreseeable and even understandable. Hornby Castle, he must have mused, was finally his. The mighty Richard had stood against him, but Stanley had won in the end.

"I Am Determined To Prove A Villain"

This line from Shakespeare's King Richard III defines the portrayal of the King that endures in the consciousness of many. Doubtless history is written by the victors but no other King was so vilified by his successors as Richard. The first cause for the desire to discredit him was Henry Tudor's own weak claim to the throne. Tudor went to great lengths not to take the Crown by right of conquest. He could not impugn Edward IV too far as he intended to marry his daughter and had relied heavily on his supporters. Richard, then, was a convenient middle man. Henry could craft an image for himself as uniting the warring Houses, ending the strife, standing as a Lancastrian heir in his own right and of having rescued the country from King Richard. In order for the last impression to stick, the country needed to feel as though it had wanted and needed to be saved from Richard.

Henry VII suffered at the hands of Richard's good reputation. York minuted the King's death in defiant term: 'King Richard, late mercifully reigning over us ... was piteously slain and murdered to the great heaviness of this city'. Two months after Bosworth the city still referred to him as 'the most famous prince of blessed memory'. Those who had not died at Bosworth, including Francis Lovell, rose twice over the next two years in an attempt to place the Earl of

Warwick on the throne. Henry was plagued by Pretenders claiming to be one of the sons of King Edward IV. Although the nobility came to terms with the new regime, as they must to protect themselves, the north in particular remained attached to the dead King in the country at large. Popular unrest as late as 1491 had Ricardian connections. Henry, then, needed to undo this.

Bishop Morton, an old foe of Richard's, eventually became Archbishop of Canterbury and had little good opinion to offer of the old King. Sir Thomas More early in the next century drew heavily upon Morton's stories for his famous History of King Richard III. In turn, these tales were immortalised by Shakespeare in his depiction of scheming, malevolent evil. Bishop Morton had begun a propaganda war upon Richard's memory with none to defend against it. King Henry had a vested interest in blackening Richard's character yet in at least one fascinating aspect he did not do so.

Richard is accused of a plethora of crimes by Shakespeare, the most famous of which is the murder of his nephews, the Princes in the Tower. The detail of this is dealt with in a separate book in this series and the general historical consensus, though far from proven, is that Richard probably did have the sons of Edward IV murdered in 1483. Certainly they disappeared whilst under his care. It is fascinating, then, that as the fledgling Tudor regime sought to paint the old King as the embodiment of evil, they never once accused him of this crime. Henry VII did not accuse him. Elizabeth Woodville never pointed the finger. In fact, Sir James Tyrell who famously did the deed in Shakespeare's tale, never confessed to the murder, though his admission has become legend.

So the new King did not attach this crime to Richard. What of Sir Thomas More? He tells the story of Tyrell's murder of the boys along with a man named John Dighton. The entire tale is, however, couched in rumour with terms such it 'it was rumoured' and 'men said'. More could not bring himself to commit to Richard's guilt. The work that More began was never finished. His nephew completed and published it after Sir Thomas's death. Did More find that there was no evidence for what he wrote? Or even that with but a little searching, the evidence pointed in a different direction?

William Shakespeare definitively and positively identifies King Richard as the murderer of his nephews, among many others. He adds the murder of Henry VI's son who died on a battlefield where Richard was present though he was not attributed with the act by contemporaries. Richard also murders the hapless Henry VI and tricks Edward into executing their brother George, a sentence which Richard appears less than pleased with in reality. Shakespeare also picks up the rumours that Richard poisoned his wife in order to marry his niece and makes them fact. What did Shakespeare have to gain by this? Royal favour certainly, but another interpretation is available.

Shakespeare paints Richard as a hunchback with a withered arm, which would have symbolised the outward manifestation of his inner corruption, and his crimes doom the nation to darkness until Henry Tudor (the current Queen's grandfather) rescues the country from disaster. The play was written early in Shakespeare's career, probably in the early 1590's. At this time the Secretary of State, later to take over his father's mantel as Lord Privy Seal, was a man called Robert Cecil. Robert's father William Cecil had been the closest advisor to Elizabeth I throughout her reign. Robert was groomed to succeed him. The Cecils were growing unpopular and Robert was later to enter secret negotiations to secure James VI of Scotland's accession to the throne as Elizabeth's successor. As she grew older, the Queen refused to name an heir and there must have been concern about what would follow the end of her illustrious reign.

In this context, Richard III's story becomes a moral tale, a warning. Robert Cecil was a hunchback. In 1588 Motley's History of the Netherlands describes Cecil as: 'A slight, crooked, hump-backed young gentleman, dwarfish in stature' and later spoke of the 'massive dissimulation (that) ... was, in aftertimes, to constitute a portion of his own character'. A scheming, dissimulating hunchback? Sound familiar? Suddenly, Shakespeare's play uses the stories of Richard III to warn the Queen of the perils of relying on Cecil's council and of the problems that can beset a country when the succession is not secured. Edward IV did not fully secure his and it resulted in a dynastic change. Was Shakespeare warning Queen Elizabeth that she risked plunging the country into a repeat of the Wars of the Roses? If she was Edward IV, Robert Cecil was Richard III scheming to replace her.

William Shakespeare was also in the entertainment game and his play is a masterpiece in the observation of evil, of fate versus free will and of the depiction of an anti-hero. We shall never know to what extent Shakespeare planned to cast in stone King Richard III's reputation or whether that was a side effect of his more current political observations.

Conclusion

So many of the facts surrounding the story of King Richard III are lost in the shadow that has been cast over him that it is hard to discern the man. Shakespeare has passed a caricature of evil into the world's consciousness with such mastery that it has become an accepted version of this man's life. What we do know of him, though, defies this one dimensional demon. He had a childhood which was certainly privileged, yet which was rocked by turbulent political events in which he was caught. Years of his development were spent buffeted by this storm from terrifying abandonment before a hostile, marauding army to spells in the uncertainty of exile. It is entirely possible that he was gripped by insecurity and so fought to make himself secure in the world and prevent his son from enduring the same problems.

Richard's motto as King was 'Loyalty Binds Me' and this appears a fitting epithet for his time spent working to secure his brother's throne and build his own son's inheritance. He was tirelessly and unflinchingly loyal and it is the odds at which this man stands with the reputation he developed during 1483 that inspires and divides those who study him today. So much of what happened during that fateful summer is wide open to vastly disparate interpretation so that two extremes can be argued from the same incident. When Richard seized his nephew, was that the first play for the throne or did he genuinely fear a Woodville plot and act in the best interests of his nephew and the country? When Lord Hastings was executed, did Richard believe him guilty of treason, plotting against his Protectorate, and act decisively, or did he ruthlessly remove Edward V's key supporter at court? Did he kill his nephews? He could struggle to be King without killing them. His own brother, their father, had taught him that lesson.

To this day, King Richard III inspires devotion from those who seek to clear his name and revulsion in others who believe that there could never be justification for his seizure of the throne and probable murder of innocent boys. King Richard III's reign is one of history's most interesting 'what if's'. How far would he have taken his social reforms? What would England have been like without the Tudors? Certainly there would have been no Henrician Reformation. Perhaps the reason that there is such strong support for him now is that he should never have been a failed King. He was betrayed at Bosworth, yet that denotes a significant failure in his character. Although he inspired fierce loyalty in those closest to him he alienated much of the aristocracy and pushed them into Tudor's welcoming arms. He marked himself as an intractable foe of France so that the old enemy sought to support a more agreeable alternative.

Was Richard the architect of his own demise? He failed to play the game of thrones well and his commitment to loyalty and chivalric values left him open to opportunism and betrayal, even making them appealing to some.

Nevertheless, he was a man, and was certainly not the pure evil he is remembered as. He had hopes, fears, dreams and tragedies. All of those ended when he lost his life in a blaze of chivalric glory at the Battle of Bosworth Field.

Further Reading

Richard the Third, Paul Murray Kendall (W.W. Norton & Company)

Richard III and the Princes in the Tower, A.J. Pollard (Bramley Books)

Richard III and the Death of Chivalry, David Hipshon (The History Press)

Eleanor The Secret Queen, John Ashdown-Hill (The History Press)

Richard III - A Medieval Kingship, Edited by John Gillingham (Collins & Brown)

Printed in Great Britain
by Amazon.co.uk, Ltd.,
Marston Gate.